PeopleSmart

PARTICIPANT WORKBOOK

Mel Silberman, Ph.D.

Freda Hansburg, Ph.D

Authors of People*Smart: Developing Your Interpersonal Intelligence*

Pfeiffer
A Wiley Imprint
www.pfeiffer.com

Copyright © 2006 by John Wiley & Sons, Inc.
Published by Pfeiffer
An Imprint of Wiley
989 Market Street, San Francisco, CA 94103-1741
www.pfeiffer.com

No part of this publication may be reproduced, stored in a retrieval system, or transmitted in any form or by any means, electronic, mechanical, photocopying, recording, scanning, or otherwise, except as permitted under Section 107 or 108 of the 1976 United States Copyright Act, without either the prior written permission of the Publisher, or authorization through payment of the appropriate per-copy fee to the Copyright Clearance Center, Inc., 222 Rosewood Drive, Danvers, MA 01923, 978-750-8400, fax 978-646-8600, or on the web at www.copyright.com. Requests to the Publisher for permission should be addressed to the Permissions Department, John Wiley & Sons, Inc., 111 River Street, Hoboken, NJ 07030, 201-748-6011, fax 201-748-6008, or online at http://www.wiley.com/go/permission.

Limit of Liability/Disclaimer of Warranty: While the publisher and author have used their best efforts in preparing this book, they make no representations or warranties with respect to the accuracy or completeness of the contents of this book and specifically disclaim any implied warranties of merchantability or fitness for a particular purpose. No warranty may be created or extended by sales representatives or written sales materials. The advice and strategies contained herein may not be suitable for your situation. You should consult with a professional where appropriate. Neither the publisher nor author shall be liable for any loss of profit or any other commercial damages, including but not limited to special, incidental, consequential, or other damages.

Readers should be aware that Internet websites offered as citations and/or sources for further information may have changed or disappeared between the time this was written and when it is read.

For additional copies/bulk purchases of this book in the U.S. please contact 800-274-4434.

Pfeiffer books and products are available through most bookstores. To contact Pfeiffer directly call our Customer Care Department within the U.S. at 800-274-4434, outside the U.S. at 317-572-3985, fax 317-572-4002, or visit www.pfeiffer.com.

Pfeiffer also publishes its books in a variety of electronic formats. Some content that appears in print may not be available in electronic books.

ISBN-10: 0-7879-7955-4
ISBN-13: 978-0-7879-7955-3

Acquiring Editor: Lisa Shannon
Director of Development: Kathleen Dolan Davies
Developmental Editor: Susan Rachmeler
Production Editor: Dawn Kilgore
Editor: Rebecca Taff
Manufacturing Supervisor: Becky Carreño
Printed in the United States of America

Printing   10 9 8 7 6 5 4 3 2 1

C O N T E N T S

Course Objectives

You will have the opportunity to . . .

- assess your skill levels for each of the eight PeopleSmart skills;
- select specific job-related situations in which you want to improve your skills;
- practice and apply three ways to develop each skill; and
- develop action plans to further practice each skill.

As a result of the course, you will come away with . . .

- greater awareness of your interpersonal strengths and weaknesses;
- inspiration to work on your interpersonal fitness; and
- immediately useful advice to get started.

Working PeopleSmart

In this module, you will have the opportunity to . . .

- examine the components of working people smart

- discuss the benefits of working people smart

- analyze the four steps to developing interpersonal intelligence

- obtain a complete profile of your people smart skills

Seven Intelligences*

Verbal	The ability to use words. Good at explaining things, likes writing and reading	*(William Shakespeare)*
Visual	The ability to see things in your mind. Good at sensing what something looks like, likes to use charts and symbols	*(Pablo Picasso)*
Physical	The ability to use your body well. Likes hands-on contact and activity	*(Michael Jordan)*
Musical	The ability to understand and use music. Remembers tunes and lyrics easily, has a natural sense of timing or rhythm, likes sounds	*(Ludwig von Beethoven)*
Mathematical and Logical	The ability to apply logic to systems and numbers. Good at analysis, calculation, planning; likes to put things in order and look for patterns	*(Albert Einstein)*
Intrapersonal	The ability to understand thoughts and feelings. Good at understanding motives. Likes quiet time to be alone in thought, reflecting about new ideas and exploring feelings	*(Sigmund Freud)*
Interpersonal	The ability to relate well to others. People smart, good at mediating and connecting. Likes contact with people, social events	*(Mother Teresa)*

---

*These intelligences were identified by Howard Gardner of Harvard University.

The Eight Essential PeopleSmart Skills

1. Understanding people

2. Expressing your thoughts and feelings clearly

3. Speaking up when your needs are not being met

4. Asking for feedback from others and giving them quality feedback in return

5. Influencing how others think and act

6. Bringing conflicts to the surface and resolving them

7. Collaborating with others, as opposed to doing things by yourself

8. Shifting gears when relationships are unproductive

Three Key Steps to Change

You've got to "WANT IT"   1

You are more likely to be motivated if you are aware of when and where you need the skill the most. Choose a situation or two in which you want to excel.

You've got to "LEARN IT"   2

Become familiar with the skills possessed by people who exemplify each of the interpersonal intelligences.

You've got to "TRY IT"   3

Most people make the mistake of going for broke and then fizzle out when results don't come quickly. By offering you some "experiments in change," we'll help you test your wings and find the initial success to sustain yourself for further practice.

WIFM (What's in it for me?)

For each of your primary relationships, first write the names of people who belong and then select two situations in which you would like to improve your people skills.

My Customers _____

_____ Understanding customers' resistance to trying new products or services

_____ Convincing customers to hear me out

_____ Eliciting feedback from customers

_____ Figuring out customers' motivation

_____ (Other): _____

My Coworkers _____

_____ Reaching consensual decisions in team meetings

_____ Understanding a difficult coworker

_____ Drawing out the views of a coworker who's quiet or new

_____ Asserting my needs with coworkers

_____ (Other): _____

My Manager _____

_____ Giving feedback to my manager

_____ Negotiating work schedules with my manager

_____ Getting my point across to my manager

_____ Getting unstuck when I feel in a rut with my manager

_____ (Other): _____

My Direct Reports _____

_____ Giving clear instructions

_____ Seeking feedback from supervisees

_____ Motivating subordinates

_____ Getting conflicts out in the open

_____ (Other): _____

Understanding People

"You can see a lot just by listening."

—Yogi Berra

In this module, you will have the opportunity to . . .

- discuss the difference between labeling people and understanding them

- assess a person who is difficult to understand to discover what makes that person tick

- practice "listening for understanding" through interviewing

- learn three ways to interpret puzzling behavior

- select "experiments in change" at work

Interpreting Behavior

Steve is arrogant, opinionated, and sloppy about his work . . . yet highly critical of others. He often makes crude or insensitive comments to people and reacts very defensively to any type of suggestion or criticism, no matter how constructive.

Steve "stumbled" onto his job at our company. Despite the training he's received, the job is a little out of his league. He knows it. And he knows that everyone else knows it. Yet he gives off an air of superiority. He won't ask for help or advice. And if help or advice is offered, he rejects it.

I JUST DON'T GET HIM.

Describe someone you "just don't get."

_____

_____

_____

_____

_____

_____

_____

_____

_____

_____

_____

_____

Five Ways to Understand People

Which of the below have you done with regard to your difficult person?

_____ 1. Take time to listen.

_____ 2. Ask questions about his or her thoughts and feelings.

_____ 3. Consult other people who may have insights about this person.

_____ 4. Try "walking in his or her shoes" by looking at events from this person's point of view.

_____ 5. Relate to the person in new ways.

Interviewing

Directions

Interview your partner about his or her Difficult Person.

- Ask questions and dig for deeper understanding.

- Solicit your partner's viewpoint (but hold back on your own).

- Seek clarification and illuminate the feelings behind what your partner is saying.

- Obtain information that hasn't been stated.

Debrief

- How did the interview go? What was challenging?

- What benefits did you and your partner experience by interviewing him or her?

How Do We Compare with Others?

Because of differences in style, gender, age, and culture, we might be very different in the following ways. *Circle* the point on each relevant continuum that fits the way you see your difficult person. Put a *square* on the point that fits the way you see yourself.

Spontaneous . . . . Careful
       *   *   *   *   *

Social . . . . Private
  *   *   *   *   *

Emotional . . . . Analytic
  *   *   *   *   *

"Take charge" . . . . Responsive
  *   *   *   *   *

Competitive . . . . Collaborative
  *   *   *   *   *

Give opinions . . . . Ask questions
  *   *   *   *   *

Intense . . . . Easygoing
  *   *   *   *   *

Focused . . . . Multitasking
  *   *   *   *   *

Confronting . . . . Avoiding
  *   *   *   *   *

Self-oriented . . . . Group-oriented
  *   *   *   *   *

Respect for talent . . . . Respect for authority
  *   *   *   *   *

Loose . . . . Rule-oriented
  *   *   *   *   *

Three Basic Needs

CONTROL
Having power over your life

CONNECTION
Inclusion, support, love

COMPETENCE
Succeeding, demonstrating mastery

How anxious is your own Difficult Person about meeting these needs?

Check any of the anxious behaviors he or she tends to exhibit:

Control
- ❑ Micromanages others
- ❑ Acts helpless and dependent
- ❑ Has great difficulty being flexible

Connection
- ❑ Rejects others
- ❑ Tries too hard to be accepted
- ❑ Seeks a lot of attention

Competence
- ❑ Brags a lot
- ❑ Puts him/herself down
- ❑ Easily becomes defensive

Working the Three C's

Below are some strategies that may help alleviate people's anxieties about **control, connection,** and **competence.** Check any that you think might be helpful to try with your difficult person.

Control

- ❏ Keep the person informed and up-to-date.
- ❏ Offer choices and decisions.
- ❏ Ask: "What role do you want (in this project)?"

Connection

- ❏ Show the person attention before he or she seeks it.
- ❏ Tactfully and directly set limits when he or she demands too much attention.
- ❏ Offer greetings or conversation in small doses.

Competence

- ❏ Give genuine positive feedback proactively.
- ❏ Don't put the person on the spot in front of others.
- ❏ Give the person a task you know he or she can do successfully.

TRY IT: Experiments in Change

Select one of the following experiments. . . .

Improving Listening:

Think of the person you consider the best listener you know, someone you invariably feel comfortable talking with. For a week, study his or her nonverbal behavior during conversations the person has with you or others. What does the person do that conveys interest and acceptance? Write down some of the behaviors you notice the person using. Next, notice whether any of these behaviors are part of your own present repertoire. If not, which of the behaviors would you be willing to try out? Choose one or two and practice them.

Decreasing Interruptions:

For a couple of days, keep a log of your conversations at work and record how often you interrupt others. You can do this informally by placing an object, such as a coin or paperclip, in a particular pocket each time you catch yourself interrupting. Calculate the percentage of your conversations that included interruptions. How do you feel about your interruption rate? If you're unhappy with it, choose a specific person or situation and, for one full day, do not interrupt at all. Notice how this makes you feel and how others respond. See whether you can identify what makes it hard for you to hear people out.

Analyzing Goals:

Think of someone you simply don't understand at all. Think about this person's behavior in a few key situations. What seems to be his or her primary goal: control, connection, or competence? Is this person's goal different from yours? When you recognize his or her usual goal, do you understand the person better? Would you change any of your own behavior in dealing with this person in the future?

Understanding Differences:

Identify someone at work who's as different as possible from you. On a 1 to 10 scale, where 1 is the lowest and 10 the highest rating, rate how well you understand this person's values, assumptions, and motivation. Now list some of the ways this person is different from you, including goals, personal style, and demographic factors. Which of these differences may be interfering with your ability to understand this person? Try to imagine yourself as this person, seeing the world through his or her eyes. How do you feel? How do things seem different to you? Now re-rate your understanding of the person. Is there a change?

Expressing Yourself Clearly

"Nothing is so simple that it cannot be misunderstood."

—Jr. Teague

In this module, you will have the opportunity to . . .

- experience when words can be confusing to others

- assess your communication skills

- identify work situations in which clear communication is essential

- practice communicating about complex subject matter

- examine the concept of "owning your communication"

- select "experiments in change" at work

Getting Invested

Two situations in which I want to improve my communication skills are . . .

❏ giving a presentation to clients on a complicated project

❏ orienting a new employee to office procedures

❏ presenting my ideas for improving an unsuccessful project to skeptical team members

❏ giving detailed instructions to a coworker

❏ conducting a performance review with a subordinate who doesn't recognize his/her work deficiencies

❏ updating my boss on the status of my projects

❏ conversing with important clients over a business lunch

❏ getting my point across to colleagues during meetings

❏ presenting my experience and qualifications during a job interview

❏ other: _____

Communicating When Things Are Complicated

Directions

- The Communicator and Receiver should sit back-to-back.

- The Receiver should not see the drawing!

- The Communicator is to describe the drawing to the Receiver so that the Receiver is able to draw it accurately.

- The Receiver may not ask questions.

- When finished, compare drawings.

- The Receiver should give feedback to the Communicator about what he or she did that was helpful or unhelpful.

Debrief

What can the Communicator do to be effective in this exercise?

Five Steps to Include the Listener

1. Orient the receiver.
2. Limit information to key points.
3. Feed information in chunks.
4. Use listener-friendly references.
5. Share the microphone.

Directions

Take turns explaining one of the following topics to your partner. Choose a topic about which you have some knowledge, but your partner does not.

- The benefits of a product or service (e.g., a new drug,)
- The features of a product or service (e.g., new operating system)
- How to _____ (e.g., a safety procedure, an activity).
- The difference between a _____ and a _____ (e.g., HMO/PPO, a PC and a MAC).
- Tips for _____ (e.g., searching the web)
- (Supply your own) _____

Debrief

1. Give your partner feedback, referring to the list of tips above.
2. Agree on how to improve your presentations.

When You Want to Be Direct

In situations where you want to speak up in a straightforward way, here are three tips to keep in mind:

Say "I," not "you."

I statements convey that you "own" your message.

Try *"I think that . . ."* rather than *"Don't you think . . ."* and *"My opinion is . . ."* rather than *"You are. . . ."*

Describe, don't blame.

Say what you think or feel in a clear, direct way instead of speaking judgmentally or sarcastically.

Try *"I disagree"* rather than *"You've got it wrong"* and *"I'm uncomfortable with the direction we're taking"* rather than *"This approach is off the wall!"*

Tell, don't hint.

Give your perspective as a statement rather than asking leading or hinting questions.

Try *"It seems to me . . ."* rather than *"Why not . . . ?"* and *"My sense is . . ."* rather than *"Haven't you noticed . . . ?"*

TRY IT: Experiments in Change

Select one of the following experiments. . . .

Owning Communication:
☐

Choose a specific work situation in which to practice making "I" statements (for example, a staff meeting). For a week, keep track of how often you speak in your own voice. Are you doing it more or less often than you want to? What makes it difficult for you to make "I" statements?

Checking for Understanding:
☐

Practice confirming understanding for a week. Whenever you've talked at length or have introduced a complicated subject, make a point of checking out the listener's understanding by asking questions such as, *"Was that clear?"* or *"So what do you think?"* Based on people's responses, would you say you're usually coming across clearly? If not, what changes could you try?

Orienting:
☐

Choose a specific assignment you want to give someone. Write, word for word, how you would explain the task to that person, incorporating the key elements of effective orientation (name and brief description of the task, example of the task, benefit of doing the task, and expected duration of the task). You may then want to try out your verbatim orientation on the person you chose, asking him or her how clear you were.

Being Straightforward:
☐

Keep a record of situations at work in which you were not up-front with someone else—when you hinted and hedged, but didn't say what was on your mind, or you brought up a different subject than the one you really wanted to raise. Think about the reasons why you were evasive. Select one or two situations that might arise again and plan how you can be more straightforward. Then try out your plan and see how it goes.

Asserting Your Needs

"Since people cannot read minds, you must tell them what you want."
—Patricia Jakubowski

In this module, you will have the opportunity to . . .

- discuss the benefits of asserting needs

- assess assertion skills

- identify work situations in which speaking up is essential

- practice assertiveness in difficult situations

- select "experiments in change" at work

Practicing Assertiveness

One situation in which I'd like to be more assertive about saying "no" or expecting someone else to do something I need is . . .

- ❑ asking my boss for help in prioritizing my workload
- ❑ dealing with excessive overtime and work travel
- ❑ refusing coworkers' requests for help with tasks that are not in my job description
- ❑ receiving slow service from a supplier
- ❑ letting a client know that his or her "humor" is offensive to me
- ❑ turning down a subordinate's request
- ❑ other: _____

What exactly do I want in this situation? How insistent am I? What reasons would I give for my refusal or request?

_____

_____

_____

_____

_____

_____

_____

_____

_____

_____

_____

_____

_____

Communicating Assertively

- Take a deep breath, slow yourself down, and talk just enough to express your wishes.

- Communicate your position, using phrases such as:

  "I would appreciate it if you . . ."

  "I will not . . ."

  "It would be great if you . . ."

  "I will have to . . ."

  "Please . . ."

  "I would prefer that you . . ."

  "It works best for me if . . ."

  "I've decided not to . . ."

- Give brief, non-apologetic explanations for your position. Stop talking after giving your reason.

  "I can't discuss it right now because I have a deadline to meet."

- Don't get defensive, caught up in power struggles, or blow your cool.

- Repeat yourself like a "broken record."

  Calmly restate what you've said.

  Say the same thing in new words.

- When you hear objections, use phrases like:

  "That may be."

  "We see it differently."

  "That's true, and. . . ."

  "I realize how important this is to you, and. . . ."

TRY IT: Experiments in Change

Select one of the following experiments. . . .

Refusing Unwanted Requests:

Make a list of requests people make of you that are a burden. Review the list and select one or two requests that you will refuse in the next week. Think about how you will politely, but firmly, inform someone of your need to say "no," then carry out your plan. What happened? Did you feel less guilty than you thought you would?

Making Clear Requests:

Review the requests you want to make of others to help you meet your own needs at work. Select one or two. Get clear in your mind what you specifically want. Formulate each request so that it is as reasonable as possible for the person you will ask, then make your request(s). Did you receive a positive response? Are you happy with the support you obtained?

Responding to Objections:

Take one of the following strategies and practice it for one week with a variety of people in various work situations. Work on it until it becomes second-nature:

- Repeat yourself rather than respond to someone's remarks.
- Avoid arguments with others by using phrases such as *"That may be," "We see it differently,"* and *"That's true, and. . . ."*
- Give brief, non-apologetic explanations for your position.

Persisting:

Work on your persistence. Identify times you give up too easily or flip-flop on an issue on a day-to-day basis. Make a small list of decisions you would like to stick to in the coming week. After the week is up, look over your list and give yourself a grade: A = stuck to my guns; B = persisted most of the time; C = persisted some of the time; D = gave up.

Exchanging Feedback

"Flatter me and I may not believe you. Criticize me and I may not like you. Ignore me and I may not forgive you. Encourage me and I will not forget you."

—William Ward Arthur

In this module, you will have the opportunity to . . .

- discuss the value of obtaining the perspectives of others

- assess feedback skills

- identify work situations in which exchanging feedback is essential

- practice giving quality feedback

- examine ways to obtain constructive feedback from others

- select "experiments in change" at work

How Many Squares?*

<table>
<tr><td></td><td></td><td></td><td></td></tr>
<tr><td></td><td></td><td></td><td></td></tr>
<tr><td></td><td></td><td></td><td></td></tr>
<tr><td></td><td></td><td></td><td></td></tr>
</table>

My answer is: _____

---

*Based on "Count the Squares," in *The Big Book of Business Games* by John Newstrom and Edward Scannell.

Partner Feedback

Directions

From the list below, select the animal that most resembles your partner, considering both physical characteristics and personal qualities. Do *not* show your selection to your partner.

- ❑ Lion

- ❑ Squirrel

- ❑ Monkey

- ❑ Tiger

- ❑ Giraffe

- ❑ Kangaroo

- ❑ Bear (type?)

- ❑ Cat (type?)

- ❑ Dog (type?)

- ❑ Bird (type?)

- ❑ Other: _____

Reasons Why People Withhold Feedback from Us

- They don't know that we really want their feedback.

- They don't know what specific feedback we are seeking.

- They don't want to hurt our feelings.

- They are concerned that we will be angry at them or seek reprisal.

- They feel they haven't earned the right to give us feedback.

Requesting Feedback

Complete the action plan below for requesting feedback from someone on the job:

The person whose feedback I'd like is: _____.
I would like that person's feedback on: _____.
The strategies I'll use to invite feedback from that person are (write down specific phrases you can use after the strategy):

❑ Give a sincere rationale for my request. _____

_____

_____

❑ Be specific about the feedback I'm seeking. _____

_____

_____

❑ Give the person time to formulate his or her feedback.

_____

_____

_____

❑ Self-assess to start the process. _____

_____

_____

❑ Find a way to make the feedback anonymous. _____

_____

_____

❑ Ask for suggestions only. _____

_____

_____

Giving Feedback

Directions

1. Discuss the checklist below with your partner:

   - Ask permission.

     "Can we talk about what happened between us at the meeting?"

     "I have some things I'd like to say to you. Is this a good time?"

   - Compliment first.

     "I appreciate your. . . ."

     "I like the way you. . . ."

   - Talk to the behavior or action, not the person. Be specific.

     "I'm concerned about the way you handled your sales call. You focused on the features of the product but not on the benefits."

   - Offer suggestions.

     "I'd like to suggest that you. . . ."

     "I think I/you/we would be more effective if you. . . ."

   - Ask for reactions.

     "Is this helpful?"

     "How do you see it?"

2. Choose someone from your work environment to whom you'd like to give feedback: _____

3. Pretend your partner is that person and practice giving him or her constructive feedback.

4. Using the points on the checklist below as a guide, tell your partner how effective his or her feedback was.

Feedback Checklist

- ❑ Asked permission?
- ❑ Complimented first?
- ❑ Talked to the behavior or action, not the person?
- ❑ Was specific?
- ❑ Offered suggestions?
- ❑ Asked for reactions?

TRY IT: Experiments in Change

Select one of the following experiments. . . .

Requesting Feedback:

Identify someone from whom you'd like to get feedback. Approach the person and say, *"I'd like to improve my [select a quality, skill, or behavior]. Could you tell me how well I'm doing right now, and also let me know in the future if there's any change for the better or worse? Could we set a time to do this?"* Evaluate the results.

Giving Feedback:

Identify two people to whom you'd like to give feedback, even if you're not sure they want it. Select one of them to whom you have never given feedback or haven't done so in a long time. Think carefully about what you will say to that person; then find an opportunity to do so. What were the results?

Giving Feedback to a Difficult Person:

Think of someone you know who seems to have difficulty accepting feedback. Write down, word for word, three ways that you might ask that person for permission to share some feedback with him or her. Then write down two positive things about the person that you could share initially to improve your chances of being heard more easily in the future.

Improving Negative Feedback:

Think of someone to whom you have recently given negative feedback. If you did not give the person suggestions for improvement, write down two things that the person could do to improve. When you next have an opportunity to speak with the person, tell him or her, *"I've been thinking about the feedback I gave you the other day, and I'm not sure I was as helpful as I could have been. Could I take a moment to explain more clearly what I meant, and try to give you some concrete suggestions?"* If the person agrees, give your improved feedback, then check out whether this was helpful to the person.

Influencing Others

"Power lasts ten years; influence not more than a hundred."

—Korean Proverb

In this module, you will have the opportunity to . . .

- experience the difficulty of overcoming resistance

- assess influence skills

- identify work situations in which you can have more impact

- learn three ways to influence others

- select "experiments in change" at work

Analyzing a Personal Case Problem

Directions

1. Think of someone you recently tried to persuade . . . without success. It may be a situation in which you wanted the person to adopt your advice, to change his or her mind, or to act in a certain way. *What were the details?*

   _____

   _____

   _____

   _____

   _____

   _____

2. Tell your partner about this experience. Then invite your partner to interview you, using these questions:

   • Did you ask questions to better understand the person's point of view?

   • Did you point out the benefits the other person would receive if he or she adopted your advice or changed his or her mind?

   • Did you give the person some time and space to mull over what you were proposing?

An Example of Influence

A supervisor was urging the toll booth collectors to be friendlier to drivers when they paid a toll. The collectors resisted. "If we talk like they do in stores and hotels these days," they argued, "the public will think we're crazy or just forced to do it. It's not what people expect." The supervisor wisely responded: "Okay, I'll make a deal with you.

"Try to say hello or say thank you or smile at the customers for one week, and we'll get back together to see if it works for you."

The next week, the toll collectors reported that they did not know what effect the experiment had on the customers, but they all reported that they liked their jobs better.

(No doubt, the customers returned their friendliness in kind.)

Practicing Influence Skills

Directions

Identify a situation from the list below or create one yourself.

1. You have been trying to convince a person who reports to you to take more initiative. That may include actions such as:

   - suggesting a better way to do something

   - when possible, undertaking a small project without waiting to be assigned to do it

   - giving you feedback about your behavior as a manager

   So far, the person has been reluctant to do this. Try to change his or her mind.

2. You want your busy boss to give you performance feedback more frequently. S/He feels that you are doing a great job and don't need the extra feedback. Your boss is also overwhelmed with his/her own responsibilities. See whether you can get the boss to commit him- or herself to what you want.

3. Someone on your team disagrees with your insistence that no important decisions are made by individuals unless they are checked out with everyone else on the team. Persuade him/her to agree with you.

4. One of your customers continues to use a service or product from another provider that you know is inferior to your own. Convince him/her to give you the business.

Ask your partner to portray the person you want to influence. Use the opportunity to practice the influence skills that have been discussed so far in this module.

When you are finished, invite your partner to give you feedback about your influence skills.

Identifying an Opportunity to Influence Others

Directions

1. Identify a situation coming up in which you want to influence someone. (It can be the same situation in which you previously failed, or a new one.) Describe it:

_____

_____

_____

_____

_____

_____

2. Consult with your partner and decide which of the following strategies you would use to influence this person. How could you use the strategy?

   - Ask questions to better understand the person's needs and concerns.
   - Point out benefits to the other person if he or she adopts your idea.
   - Give the person time and space to consider your proposal.
   - Use a "foot in the door" strategy:

     Ask the person to listen to your views without pressure to respond.

     Invite the person to read something.

     Encourage a one-time experiment.

     Urge the person to consider a small action.

TRY IT: Experiments in Change

Select one of the following experiments. . . .

Developing Rapport:

Make it a special project to take time to develop rapport with someone you want to influence. Think about how to show interest in that person. Also, think of how you can be more interesting to him or her. Avoid giving advice during this time. Develop trust by letting the person see that you are not out to remake him or her in your image. Also, accentuate the positive. Seize every opportunity to compliment the person. It's hard to influence someone you have criticized a lot.

Asking Questions:

Think of two people you want to influence as your "customers." Devote a week to working on asking questions rather than giving advice. Learn more about their needs, preferences, and wishes, and store that information for later use.

Practicing Patience:

For one week, try to lessen your eagerness to influence people right away. Every time you are in a situation in which you want to be persuasive, try to be patient with yourself and with others. Give yourself time to think before you speak, and give others the space and elbow room to consider what you're saying without responding right away. See whether you like the results.

Being Persuasive:

Identify a person to whom you want to be more persuasive. Develop a plan for encouraging that person to accept your idea. Prepare yourself with information about the benefits of your ideas. Think about how you might make your suggestions more appealing by using good examples, re-framing, and metaphors. Try out your plan.

Resolving Conflict

"As long as you keep a person down, some part of you has to be down there to hold him down, so it means you cannot soar as you otherwise might."

—Marian Anderson

You will have the opportunity to . . .

- examine feelings about conflict and preferences for dealing with it

- assess conflict resolution skills

- identify work situations in which conflict resolution is essential

- examine ways to understand the interests of the other side and use them to create resolution

- practice win-win conflict resolution

- select "experiments in change" at work

Comfort with Conflict

Directions

1. Circle the number below that describes how comfortable you are with conflict most of the time:

Uncomfortable . . . . Comfortable

| 1 | 2 | 3 | 4 | 5 |

2. Discuss with your partner what makes you comfortable and uncomfortable in conflict situations.

3. Thumb wrestle with your partner until one of you wins two out of three rounds.

4. Based on your thumb wrestling experience, answer the following questions:

   - Who liked it?

   - Who disliked it?

   - Who was competitive?

   - Who was sneaky?

   - Who was defensive?

   - Who was easygoing?

Four Styles of Conflict

CONFRONTATIONAL people tend to be aggressive, "in your face" types who can be bullying or judgmental.

PERSUASIVE individuals are assertive and don't hesitate to stand up for themselves.

COOPERATIVE types are comfortable doing more listening than talking. They are often willing to be conciliatory, but will speak up if an issue is important to them.

AVOIDING people would prefer to cross the street rather than engage in a conflict. They may withdraw or accept situations they dislike, rather than speak up.

In order to handle conflicts effectively, it's important to expand our range of styles and to recognize the styles we encounter in others that may pose difficulty for us.

My conflict style is usually:

_____ with my coworkers

_____ with my manager

_____ with my customers

_____ with my direct reports

Handling the Four Styles of Conflict

Confrontational

Don't give in to intimidation. Calmly ask the person to "lower the volume" (*"I think we'll do better if we slow down and hear each other out"*).

Persuasive

Acknowledge the person's points without abandoning your own interests (*"What you're saying makes good sense. Perhaps you haven't also considered that . . ."*).

Cooperative

Draw out additional concerns the person may have, in addition to sharing your own (*"Is there anything else that's important to you that we haven't touched on?"*).

Avoiding

Create a safe environment for sharing needs and concerns (*"As an experiment, could we spend the next five minutes imagining what each of us would walk away with in the best of all possible worlds?"*).

Role for Dr. Roland in the Ugli Orange Case*

You are Dr. P. W. Roland. You work as a research biologist for a pharmaceutical firm. The firm is under contract with the government to do research on methods to combat enemy uses of biological warfare.

Recently several World War II experimental nerve gas bombs were moved from the United States to a small island just off the U.S. coast in the Pacific. During transportation, two of the bombs developed leaks. The leaks are presently controlled, but government scientists believe the gas will permeate the bomb chambers within two weeks. They know of no method to prevent the gas from reaching the atmosphere and spreading to other islands, and very likely the West Coast as well. If this occurs, thousands of people will incur serious brain damage or die.

You've developed a synthetic vapor, which will neutralize the nerve gas if it is injected into the bomb chambers before the gas leaks out. The vapor is made with a chemical taken from the rind of the Ugli orange, a very rare fruit. Unfortunately, only 3,000 of these oranges were produced this season.

You have learned that a Mr. R. H. Cardoza, a fruit exporter in South America, is in possession of 3,000 Ugli oranges. The chemicals from the rinds of this number of oranges would be sufficient to neutralize the gas if the serum is developed and injected efficiently. You have also been informed that the rinds of these oranges are in good condition.

You have also learned that Dr. J. W. Jones is also urgently seeking purchase of Ugli oranges and is aware of Mr. Cardoza's possession of the 3,000 oranges available. Dr. Jones works for a firm with which your firm is highly competitive. There is a great deal of industrial espionage in the pharmaceutical industry. Over the years, your firm and Dr. Jones' firm have frequently sued each other for violations of industrial espionage laws and infringement of patent rights. Litigation is still in progress.

The Federal government has asked your firm for assistance. You've been authorized by your firm to approach Mr. Cardoza to purchase the 3,000 Ugli oranges. You have been told he will sell them to the highest bidder and your firm has authorized you to bid as high as $2 million to obtain the rind of the oranges. Before approaching Mr. Cardoza, you have decided to talk with Dr. Jones to influence him so that he will not prevent you from purchasing the oranges.

---

*Used with the permission of Robert J. House.

Role for Dr. Jones in the Ugli Orange Case*

You are Dr. John W. Jones, a biological research scientist employed by a pharmaceutical firm. You have recently developed a synthetic chemical useful for curing and preventing Rudosen, a disease contracted by pregnant women. If not caught in the first four weeks of pregnancy, Rudosen causes serious brain, eye, and ear damage to the unborn child. Recently, there has been an outbreak of Rudosen in your state and several thousand women have contracted the disease.

You have found, with volunteer victims, that your recently developed synthetic serum cures Rudosen in its early stages. Unfortunately, the serum is made from the juice of the Ugli orange, a very rare fruit. Only a small quantity, 3,000 of these oranges, were produced last season. No additional Ugli oranges will be available until next season, too late to cure the present Rudosen victims.

You've demonstrated that your synthetic serum is in no way harmful to pregnant women and it has no side effects. The Food and Drug Administration has approved the production and distribution of the serum as a cure for Rudosen. The present outbreak was unexpected and your firm had not planned on having the compound serum available for six months. Your firm holds the patent on the synthetic serum and it is expected to be a highly profitable product when it becomes generally available to the public.

You have recently been informed that Mr. R. H. Cardoza, a South American fruit exporter, is in possession of 3,000 Ugli oranges in good condition. If you could obtain the juice of all 3,000, you would be able to cure the present victims and provide sufficient inoculation for the remaining pregnant women in the state.

You have also learned that Dr. P. W. Roland is also urgently seeking Ugli oranges and is also aware of Mr. Cardoza's possession of the 3,000 oranges available. Dr. Roland is employed by a competitor pharmaceutical firm and has been working on biological warfare research for the past several years. There is a great deal of industrial espionage in the pharmaceutical industry. Over the years, Dr. Roland's firm and your firm have repeatedly sued each other for violation of industrial espionage laws and patent infringement. Litigation is still in progress.

You've been authorized by your firm to approach Mr. Cardoza to purchase the 3,000 Ugli oranges. You have been told he will sell them to the highest bidder. Your firm has authorized you to bid as high as $2 million to obtain the juice of the 3,000 available oranges. Before approaching Mr. Cardoza, you have decided to talk with Dr. Roland to influence him so that he will not prevent you from purchasing the oranges.

---

*Used with the permission of Robert J. House.

Getting to Win/Win

1. Agree on your differences.

   "We seem to disagree about _____."

   "We've been fighting about _____ for quite a while."

   "As I understand it, you want _____ and I want _____. Would you agree?"

2. Focus on needs, not positions.

   "Let me explain what concerns me and you tell me what concerns you."

3. Ask questions.

   "What's important to you?"

   "What would you do if you were in my shoes?"

   "How did you come up with that position?"

   "What else is important to you?"

4. Offer possible solutions.

   "Let's come up with some ideas together."

   "Would that idea work?"

   "What's our best idea?"

   "What exactly are we going to do? When?"

Questions for Understanding Needs

1. Review the list of sample conflict situations below. Either choose one that fits your experience or describe a conflict situation of your own:
   - ❑ Conflict in an office with a coworker who has not behaved in a professional manner
   - ❑ Conflict with a manager or coworker over a specific action plan or strategy for increasing business
   - ❑ Conflict with direct reports on timeliness or organizational matters
   - ❑ Conflict with a supplier over deliveries
   - ❑ Conflict within a team over procedures
   - ❑ Conflict with your manager over work/life balance issues
   - ❑ Conflict with representatives from other companies over competitive practices
   - ❑ Conflict within teams over inequities in work schedules
   - ❑ Conflict with direct reports over quality of work
   - ❑ Other: _____
     _____

2. Review the list of questions below and select the ones you would use to understand the other person's needs in your own situation:
   - ❑ What do you want?
   - ❑ Why do you want that?
   - ❑ What's concerning you?
   - ❑ What would you do if you were in my shoes?
   - ❑ What makes that seem fair to you?
   - ❑ What's the most important part of that for you?
   - ❑ How would that benefit you?
   - ❑ How did you come up with that position?
   - ❑ What else matters to you in this situation?

Conflict Worksheet

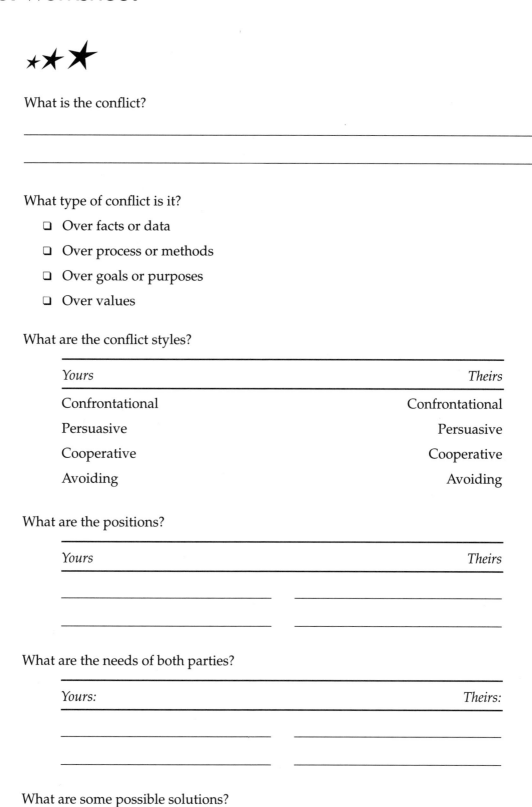

What is the conflict?

_____

_____

What type of conflict is it?

- ❑ Over facts or data
- ❑ Over process or methods
- ❑ Over goals or purposes
- ❑ Over values

What are the conflict styles?

Yours	Theirs
Confrontational	Confrontational
Persuasive	Persuasive
Cooperative	Cooperative
Avoiding	Avoiding

What are the positions?

Yours	Theirs

What are the needs of both parties?

Yours:	Theirs:

What are some possible solutions?

_____

_____

TRY IT: Experiments in Change

Select one of the following experiments. . . .

Describing a Conflict:

Identify a longstanding disagreement you have been having with someone. How have you been defining the problem? See whether you can state the problem in mutual terms such as, *"The conflict we are having is . . ."* or *"Our conflict is. . . ."* Do the issues look different when you frame the conflict this way? Decide what type of conflict you are having with this person. Is it over facts, methods, purposes, or values? Are there any different approaches to the conflict you might take, based on your analysis?

Analyzing Conflict Style:

Identify your own usual style of dealing with conflict. Are you primarily confrontational, persuasive, cooperative, or avoiding? List some examples of conflict situations in which you relied on this particular style. What were the consequences? Choose an alternative style you might have used in each of these situations. What would you have done differently?

Identifying Interests:

Select a current or recent conflict you have been dealing with. Write down the positions taken by you and the other party. Now brainstorm your own interests in the situation, as well as those of the other party. Have these issues been addressed at all in your efforts to resolve the conflict? How might you put them on the table?

Brainstorming Solutions:

Choose a current conflict situation and brainstorm as many mutual gain options as you can. Do you think any of these solutions might be workable? Consider sharing your list with the other party and inviting the person to add his or her own ideas.

Being a Team Player

"Ask not what your teammates can do for you. Ask what you can do for your teammates."

—Magic Johnson

In this module, you will have the opportunity to . . .

- discuss the challenges of being a team player

- assess collaboration skills

- identify work situations in which collaboration is essential

- examine three ways to promote teamwork

- practice team facilitation

- select "experiments in change" at work

Some Lessons from "Broken Squares"

- It's crucial to be aware of the needs (or "job") of others, as well as your own.

- Teamwork is hampered when there is little or no communication.

- You have to be patient in teams. It takes time for things to come together.

- You may figure things out individually before others. It's frustrating when you can't simply tell people what to do, but it may be necessary not to do so to give them the opportunity to do it themselves.

- Sometimes, for the good of the team, you may have to start over again.

- There is a thrill in team accomplishment.

Things Team Players Do

Read and discuss the following list of things team players do:

1. Assist someone else when appropriate.

2. Ask quiet or new teammates for their opinions.

3. Facilitate a discussion with teammates who are in conflict.

4. Share credit you receive for a job well done.

5. Check to see how your decisions might affect others.

6. Include everyone in the information loop.

7. Seek information and expertise of others.

8. Inform others what they can do to support your efforts and ask them to tell you when they need help.

From the list, identify two actions you see as especially important in your work situation:

A. _____

B. _____

Building a Climate of Dialogue

We use the expression "everyone is entitled to his or her own opinion" when we want to support freedom of speech. However, there are social limits to this right in team situations. Too often, team discussion becomes a debate of my idea versus your idea. People advocate for the causes dear to their hearts, hoping to gain support from others. The climate becomes very politicized. By contrast, when a climate of dialogue exists, team members listen to each other, react to and build on each other's ideas, and look for and acknowledge real differences of opinion. Dialogue means "two minds together." The purpose of dialogue is to enlarge ideas, not diminish them. Here are ways you can help to build a climate of dialogue:

- Ask questions to clarify what others are saying.

- Invite others to seek clarification of your ideas.

- Share what's behind your ideas. Reveal your assumptions and goals. Invite others to do so in kind.

- Ask others to give you feedback about your ideas.

- Give constructive feedback about the ideas of others.

- Make suggestions that build on the ideas of others.

- Incorporate the ideas of others into your proposals.

- Find common ground among the ideas expressed in the group.

- Encourage others to give additional ideas from those already expressed.

Winter Survival

You have just crash-landed in the woods of northern Minnesota. It is 11:32 a.m. in mid-January. The light plane in which you were traveling crashed on a lake. The pilot and copilot were killed. Shortly after the crash, the plane sank completely into the lake with the pilot's and copilot's bodies inside. None of you are seriously injured and you are all dry.

The crash came suddenly, before the pilot had time to radio for help or inform anyone of your position. Since your pilot was trying to avoid a storm, you know the plane was considerably off course. The pilot announced shortly before the crash that you were twenty miles northwest of a small town that is the nearest known habitation.

You are in a wilderness area made up of thick woods broken by many lakes and streams. The snow depth varies from above the ankles in windswept areas to knee-deep where it has drifted. The last weather report indicated that the temperature would reach minus 25 degrees Fahrenheit in the daytime and minus 40 at night. There is plenty of dead wood and twigs in the immediate area. You are dressed in winter clothing appropriate for wear in Washington, D.C. (your departure city) and Seattle (your destination).

While escaping from the plane, you were able to salvage the twelve items listed below. You may assume that the number of passengers is the same as the number of persons in your group. **Your group has agreed to stick together.**

With these resources, develop a plan for survival.

- Ball of steel wool
- Newspapers (one per person)
- Compass
- Ax
- Cigarette lighter (no fluid)
- Loaded .45 caliber pistol
- Sectional air map
- 20 × 20 foot piece of heavy-duty canvas
- Extra shirts and pants for all
- Can of shortening
- Quart of 100-proof whiskey
- Family-size chocolate bar (one per person)

Real-World Problem Solving

Directions

1. Your group's task is to find solutions to the problem:

   _____

   _____

   _____

2. First, record your own "out of the box" ideas on Post-it Notes (one idea per note). Post your completed ideas on the wall.

3. Bring an index card and review the "gallery of ideas." Write down on the card ideas that seem worthwhile.

4. Using your notes from the "gallery," hold a team discussion, taking turns facilitating as directed.

Debrief

1. What will you do with your ideas?

2. What facilitation behaviors were helpful?

TRY IT: Experiments in Change

Select one of the following experiments. . . .

Identifying Teamwork Opportunities:

Make a list of things you do independently of others at work. Examine the list and identify items for which it would be helpful if you involved others rather than doing things alone.

Improving Group Process:

If you are a member of a group that you would like to see improve, suggest using interactive discussion formats and creative approaches to problem solving. Identify roles that you could play to help facilitate teamwork, such as heading a subcommittee, publishing group accomplishments, or even leading a meeting.

Improving Decision Making:

Think about how your work team makes decisions. Is it by voting? Do powerful members express their preferences and everyone else simply goes along? Talk up the advantages of reaching decisions by consensus. Listen to people's concerns about the time required and other issues. Suggest ways these concerns can be alleviated.

Incorporating Minority Opinions:

Observe how minority opinion is dealt with in your team meetings. Are people with dissenting opinions brushed aside? Identify specific steps you can take to help the group hear from the minority.

Shifting Gears

"If you never budge, don't expect a push."

—Malcolm Forbes

In this module, you will have the opportunity to . . .

- discuss the challenges of shifting gears

- assess shifting gears skills

- identify work situations in which shifting gears is essential

- examine two ways to shift gears

- practice changing tactics in difficult situations

"Cross Out the Letters"

Directions

Cross out six letters so that the remaining letters, without altering their sequence, spell a familiar English word.

B S A I N X L E A T N T E A R S

An Example of Shifting Gears

Harry was dismayed that his suggestions were rarely taken seriously by his boss. When he evaluated the situation, he realized that, once rebuffed, he would lie low for a while, even for days at a time, before offering new ideas. Harry decided to give suggestions more frequently, even if they were rejected. Each time he was rebuffed, he graciously accepted the rejection with the comment, "Maybe my next idea will be better." This change in tactics still led nowhere, but Harry noticed that each time he made a suggestion, the boss made more of an effort to explain why it would not work for him. Next, he noticed that his boss would sometimes act on one of Harry's suggestions without saying so. Although Harry wanted credit where it was due, he nonetheless was grateful that he was starting to have an impact on his boss. It wasn't until weeks later that Harry's boss finally began thanking him for his ideas.

Getting Unstuck

Directions

1. Identify a relationship in which you feel a need to get unstuck:

    _____ Your boss

    _____ One of your customers

    _____ One of your direct reports

    _____ One of your teammates or coworkers

2. Figure out what's stuck in this situation. Evaluate the dynamics of the relation-ship. Ask yourself questions such as:

    • Am I too enmeshed with this person? Do I need to back off and give him/her more space?

    • Are we too disengaged? Do I need to communicate more often with this person or give him/her more support?

    Analyze differences in style between you and the other person. Consider:

    • Do we have different styles? To what extent is each of us inclined to be . . .

    > concerned with facts and logic

    > friendly and empathic

    > comfortable taking charge

    > enthusiastic and impulsive

    Assess how your interactions with this person typically go.

    • What behaviors do each of you keep repeating nearly every time you are stuck on something?

    The other person's behavior: _____

    _____

    _____

    Your response: _____

    _____

    _____

3. Act in novel ways. Consider some new approaches you might take with the other person. Choose one or two and test the waters for a few days or weeks. If your experiment shows signs of success, make a commitment to the changes you have made. Review the actions below:

   ❑ Take extra time to build rapport and establish trust with this person.

   ❑ Be firmer and more consistent about what you expect from this person.

   ❑ Take a positive approach by reinforcing and encouraging this person.

   ❑ Ask the person to tell you about his or her views, needs, and concerns.

   ❑ Back off on a big change; focus on little ones.

   ❑ Be more honest and straight with this person about what you think and feel.

   ❑ Be more persistent with your efforts to influence this person.

PeopleSmart Day-by-Day

"It does not matter how slowly you go, so long as you do not stop."

—Confucius

In this module, you will have the opportunity to . . .

- review the eight skills

- develop an action plan for the next month

- arrange with a partner for follow-up

- reflect on what you've learned

Reviewing Working PeopleSmart

$100

The first PeopleSmart skill is

- ❏ Avoiding trouble
- ❏ Exchanging feedback
- ❏ Understanding people
- ❏ Letting it all hang out

$200

Resolving conflict effectively involves

- ❏ Win/lose solutions
- ❏ Lose/lose solutions
- ❏ Win/win solutions
- ❏ Arguing

$500

Being a team player does not involve

- ❏ Patience
- ❏ Collaboration
- ❏ Sharing the credit
- ❏ Constant fun

$1,000

Besides giving feedback to others, it's important to

- ❏ Ask them for money
- ❏ Let them know they are helpless
- ❏ Leave as soon as possible
- ❏ Ask them for feedback about yourself

$2,000

The best way to assert yourself is to

- ❑ Be loud
- ❑ Remain calm and confident
- ❑ Apologize first
- ❑ Justify your actions

$4,000

A good way to understand others is

- ❑ To give them psychological tests
- ❑ To look at how you compare to them
- ❑ To give them feedback
- ❑ To trust your gut

$8,000

The percentage of people fired for poor interpersonal skills is

- ❑ 60 percent
- ❑ 98 percent
- ❑ 76 percent
- ❑ 90 percent

$16,000

To shift gears, it may be helpful to

- ❑ Try a new approach, even when you're in the right
- ❑ Examine who started you off in the wrong direction
- ❑ Use trial and error
- ❑ Take a vacation

$32,000

Which is not a good way to include the listener?

- ❑ Feed information in chunks
- ❑ Repeat yourself like a broken record
- ❑ Give the big picture first
- ❑ Share the microphone

$64,000

The seven intelligences do not include

- ❑ Introspection
- ❑ Visual acuity
- ❑ Logical reasoning
- ❑ People smarts

$250,000

The best thing to do if you have a strong need to give advice is to

- ❑ Slow yourself down
- ❑ Drop your agenda for a while
- ❑ Manage your emotions
- ❑ Make your points more compelling

$500,000

Who was *not* quoted in this course?

- ❑ Marion Anderson
- ❑ Patricia Jakubowski
- ❑ Yogi Berra
- ❑ Steven Forbes

$1,000,000

The most consistently important PeopleSmart behavior is to

- ❑ Go through the front door instead of the back door
- ❑ Ask questions
- ❑ Tell others what's in it for them
- ❑ Give a sincere rationale

A Checklist of PeopleSmart Actions

Look over the list below and select one action from each category that is the most important for you to take.

TO UNDERSTAND PEOPLE BETTER . . .

- ❑ ask more questions
- ❑ avoid labeling
- ❑ look beyond surface behavior
- ❑ evaluate how I compare to another person (style, gender, age, culture)

TO EXPRESS MYSELF MORE CLEARLY . . .

- ❑ think before I talk
- ❑ provide more/less detail
- ❑ "give up the microphone"
- ❑ be straightforward and direct

TO ASSERT MY NEEDS BETTER . . .

- ❑ get clearer about what I want
- ❑ say no when I must
- ❑ speak up and ask for what I need
- ❑ remain calm and confident under fire

TO EXCHANGE FEEDBACK BETTER . . .

- ❑ invite others to give me feedback
- ❑ listen to the feedback others give me
- ❑ don't withhold feedback I can give
- ❑ offer suggestions instead of criticism

TO BECOME MORE INFLUENTIAL . . .

- ❑ temporarily drop my agenda and connect
- ❑ find out more about the opinions of others
- ❑ explain the benefits others may obtain
- ❑ give people time to mull over my advice

TO RESOLVE CONFLICTS MORE EFFECTIVELY . . .

- ❑ bring concerns out into the open sooner
- ❑ find out what the other party needs
- ❑ seek solutions, not victory
- ❑ persevere despite initial negative reactions

TO BECOME A BETTER COLLABORATOR . . .

- ❑ find out what teammates need
- ❑ express appreciation
- ❑ use the talents of others
- ❑ keep others informed about my activity

TO SHIFT GEARS, WHEN NECESSARY . . .

- ❑ accept when a relationship is in a rut
- ❑ look for the patterns we fall into
- ❑ take the initiative in shifting gears
- ❑ do something different

Notes